All is not yet lost

These poems gather in a kind of aftermath, as characters, as shadows of events, stalking late night deserted streets. In the flickering of debris. The body that 'used to could' hovers about the poems in a strange death: a silence before the cycle of human endeavor resets— 'my will become rock.' I marvel at what Fagin can do in the space of a line, what she hears of the world, how she re-shuffles what she hears, making beautiful truncated structures that you will want to underline, to post, to score into a wall.

—RENEE GLADMAN

Betsy Fagin's poems seem to operate under and above this world's bent surfaces and shadowy infrastructures, teasing out its harrowing, occasionally loving idiosyncrasies from intimate distances. It's like the poems know what's been superimposed onto reality to play at reality, and they speak from curious, tough, funny and live-sounding breaks to expose—and handle—the cracks in the game. I've admired Fagin's ability to place words in clear, elusive, instructional and cosmically present and afflicted roles—without telegraphing any of those roles—for a long time. It's a real pleasure to finally get a longer run of her work in one place.

—ANSELM BERRIGAN

Betsy Fagin's *All is not yet lost*, is a luminous love letter to revolution, of resistance to a slow death in capitalism's arms. The poems delve into the fatal disconnect between capitalism's cold heart and humanity's hot, beating one. Fagin fearlessly reclaims language, space, and ourselves; this book is a song for office and kitchen workers as well as a challenge to the powers that be.

—BRENDA COULTAS

ISBN: 978-0-9885399-2-1

Cover, interior design, and typesetting by HR Hegnauer.

Belladonna* is a reading and publication series that pro-
motes the work of women writers who are adventurous,
experimental, politically involved, multiform, multi-cul-
tural, multi-gendered, impossible to define, delicious to
talk about, unpredictable, & dangerous with language.
Belladonna* is supported by funds granted by the New
York State Council on the Arts, the O Books Fund, and
from generous donations from our supporters.

NYSCA

Library of Congress Cataloging-in-Publication Data

    Fagin, Betsy.
     [Poems. Selections]
     All is not yet lost / Betsy Fagin.
       pages cm
     Includes bibliographical references.
     ISBN 978-0-9885399-2-1
     I. Title.
     PS3606.A2657A6 2015
     811'.6--dc23

Distributed to the trade by
Small Press Distribution
1341 Seventh Street
Berkeley, CA 94710
www.SPDBooks.org

Also available directly through
Belladonna*
925 Bergen Street, Suite 405
Brooklyn, NY 11238
www.BelladonnaSeries.org

* deadly nightshade, a cardiac and respiratory stimulant, having
purplish-red flowers and black berries.

All is not yet lost

Betsy Fagin

BELLADONNA* 2015

it's going to be all right

how can this be?
sleep increase pressure.
laughing knows why.
garbage heart. thrown out. take to want.

clothed dumpstered consciousness in body
choreograph the hottest blood.
my good eye. seagull crawl, raven thought.
hawk away. geese gone solitary.

pigeon music. sweet starling music.
ace me. serve nothing, time still passed.
the plague has patterns of old feeding habits
plunge tides this way, cheapened hope.

you better move. to right it. get to bass-heavy:
any song you want. galactically—
you mad? we entertain philosophies of flawless sky
reflected in rivers from higher ground.

air firewater crossroads experience
ourselves falling for amazement.
denied weakening. alight. inspired.
worth security down. nailed to apprehension time.

to strive a thing attachments offer too much
burst this eyes whole days for sleep.
my dry well candle spectacle:
free dream food.

FROM Narcissus and Echo

they are stone.
hear viscerally
thrill-charged
unruled, displaced.
harboring relentless voice
to bone voice capture.

hidden disgrace,
numb to ice water
for advance if echo.
yet looking just
fired up enough:
so small and worn out.

give back every hour
of corporate want
undone body to voice
machine explanations
that ring throughout
the streets: everybody wins.

the signs, all stolen.
investments crazed
for clear water:
the better
to inspire to heights
to nice and clean

and well-contained.
reluctant space funneled
sea foam into seat cushions
inflated, the sun
just so. in the heavens.
well-behaved. my heart,

trained, secured.
pack leader.
tracked. in love
with experts
across the forests
of Brooklyn and Queens.

as we all

stopped short,
utterly dismayed.
there, loaded and then
another of him,

a lesser him—clearly a castoff—
unfortunates
encountered each other
made forceful

through the dramatic
hopes of preventing, nope,
Too Late. the worse for regret.
and mildly horrified.

I began to understand.
as more was discarded,
more was diminished by
the encounter.

excitement of life itself drained—
hung low. withered.
all humor disappeared.
disappointment

no longer denied
but stuck:
accelerated process
danced across everyone's face.

this couldn't be good or the pure
wisdom of chance: office workers
getting off wandered around
the reading room—passaged

to little effect.
I expected to see change.
new acquisitions or upcoming
programs. the worst of the traffic

approaching city limits as
the front line of the battle
is the hottest. I want to be
your lover in real life.

this is both a visible weakness
and debilitating fear for me.
even when I am king
I will have set no goals.

someone here right now
wants to meet banks, corporate
cathedrals. grains of sand
along the road into any city

are everyone's central mind
reaching the formal terminal.
our interstellar dripping off
and forming pools

all around the chairs in which we "sat."
sitting in a despised city,
knowing no other.
our survival imagined us.

the formula worked. it worked!
let's add a noir kiss in post.
for the heart is where treasure
is always stored.

a light breeze thrills
embroidered curtains
as do I. as the walls breathe—
as we all.

thin tendrils, vine surround
as though purple and black magic
sprout near midnight creak
where are gatherings,

watchful from secretly
tuned gold for dancing.
fire-naked took
as plow, hold tight.

this love's not real

all I want

from you

is your

corporation

all I wanna do

going attentive is the same
as paying more to have.
the move to convergence
won't come undone: lifetimes
of protocols get old and take
a turn through the grid industry.

ideas change. patterns stop.
nature demands, irascible.
everybody gets emotional:
building a competitive world
of melted demand doesn't bother me,
but scares the kids.

exploring wide open fields
of no secret. transmission used
to be across wires, dogging us.
a nurturing side signals capacity
to figure out what's going on
within the self. like extra intelligence

to the edges. the annex is wiped out
from the flood: the next annex.
error detection repeats
cosmopression—hot feet, work to do,
repeating algorithms in her sleep—
capacity blown.

used techniques to challenge
overlord qualities. makes lives much easier.
scenery floods built-in sophistications.
injection in multiple streams.
the new weather centers await time-
keepers for their stores of wealth;

deteriorating backups of backups
with no place to run.
I will diagnose myself.
both memory space and workload
shared: pilled-out but still strong,
I name myself Protect.

thread a desperate love. vetted
water is cement on impact. warning
waves beacon though I didn't realize it
at the time, the treatment serves
as a message communicated
through plastic restraints. now safe

from harm if uncomfortable.
aglow from my sword
capability. tyrant distance.
discovered seeds from apple
traffickers connected through
promiscuous listening.

resolved

did you play in the rain
sad creature?
wading in once
moving from any city
to want sleep
or running the risk
of heavens' impossible
season charmed out
of their homes
dun night blinded
creation's authentic fabric
with impostors, local.
a costume of little
being left refined
prayers beneath finally
mincing possible singing
overlaid rainy flight
banished broke
from discovery sea,
freed behind a lovely
marriage of found words,
dry meaning, and
exacting music upended
pleasing smiles around
everything said. you watch,
make a lot of dismal
resolutions.

new old forest: infrastructure

I used to believe in humans
who seized death by a thousand cuts

who see the dry season as looking
for water and the wet season as rinsed clean.

that's one less car to steal
the doormats and break all the windows

with menacing lead pipes and heaps
of trash piled up: dis con indeed.

I dread crumbling sidewalks and urine-soaked
floors where all the books are ruined.

where women in huts communicate only
by clapping—one for yes, two for no—beading

accessories to sell to street shoppers for relief.
for door prizes. for these reasons,

resistance is beautiful and looks
not as trashy as it could under that trenchcoat

or at the forest banquet where welded chandeliers
and roaring fires in stone pits leave us gnawed on.

leave overflowed cornucopia of fruits and nut meats
on the clothed table. ripped-out hearts preserved

in jars of bottled hetch hetchy water, distract
any afternoon parlor from its velvet cushions for tea.

new old forest of forgiveness

assume the landscape of nightmare:
our monstrous lives terrifying
whole nations with malicious intent.
along with our violent control of curiosity.

just wanting you to be happy
in your little bed right next to mine.

no, this will never really work
but here's why

at last we are agreed!
expectation crowned
with desire to meet limitation—

all names & numbers point to pride,
to tangible rewards and predators
singing in the country voices

of welcome, dire beauty, only for you.
rife with struggle, sick in a corner, sulking.
in all that they do, they prosper.

wonder trampled, smiled to appear
more friendly. licks lips to show availability,
desirability to the audience.

it doesn't mean what it looks like.
burning in the tunnels for heat
while dissent rise up outside

the palace whose maps and outlines
of waterfalls and wide open spaces
are only high ceilings and manicured gardens

with organized pebble paths,
well-groomed hedges and still
breathable city air. past the fences

was error, anomaly. one great big mistake.
these higher buildings, close together
with delicate footprints: the higher

they climb the easier to even
higher, to shake though we sword no oath.
not even to lovers' repair or reinforcement

against stomach fuckup and heart hurts
against teardrop repeat. teardrop remix.
restless though there's nothing wrong

with what we do. nothing wrong
with us. each constitutes through
the other—no self, just relation

between I'm sorry
and I don't care.
untold desires work our will.

glass heart

have infiltrated headquarters of arch enemy.
must acquire. must accomplish data center.
must superlative. enter. pacing corridors, advance!
air shaft. HVAC system meets standards, check.

the heating and cooling of central units will be our aim,
our cover. voting systems of all kinds outlawed.
runaways collected by dragging streams. combing forests
with massive nets. devices. tracking, tracing. uncovering.

night turns into day. the forward thinking have masked
themselves to fit seamlessly into accepted realities.
image projected match image expected.
former glories encased in bubbling plastics.

fail-safe

over-appreciation detection—
butterfly threat
sharply felt restraint

of imposition rivers astonished.
altered two thousand years
of ephemera, recruited endless

agitation disastrous
then crucial:
more inner hauntings.

implicit acceptance of viciousness—
it's mine, all mine.
dusty, but non-dualistic.

tired tapestry compromise—
wall coverings—awakened
for spring. upon this star.

entangled, fascinating:
flawlessly, time and space
organized chaos.

loss and diminish.
neglect and distort.
eyes look potential,

realized clay, chalk,
dust—time's waste.
the drowned eye, a treasure.

never not broken

for Akhilandeshvari

dire beauty fallen
into obligation   dark
round   true cross quarters

one of the four gates
diving   in the way of
letting it all hang out.

tired   youth's lit candle
ritual—   passing on nearness
to mysterious forces

we have come, dour,
to make the song world
of disbelief   more beauty.

awakened unpretty,
non-decorative power.
agent of decay   to roots

rebirth. ally of
transformative. a living
          sensed,   asleep.

we don't normally do
solution.   found any
being a light.

arise! dream the occasion.
while the city sleeps
the rest of you, inked, will die.

awaken what years ago
was   called love.
we should have each other.

imagination + daring action.
we slip   transformed
broken into beauty and joy.

graceful degradation

flow. to ceiling. to tread
water. neither blessing nor curse—
mechanical nature's complexity

means fragility rolling alongside
equilibrium. resist
may forces and their dampened hearts.

take their technology.
prevent continuous need,
territorial embrace.

adapt past obsolescence
clinging to structure's
constant resistance.

collective global

let me go.
release this horizon moment of certainty.
offerings of sweet relief fuel no flame, expend
themselves in effort. the entire community is at stake.

its dour sounds crated, shipped by van then boat
from here to Argentina. packed in the open newsletters
that formulate opinion while unable to answer
even their own most basic questions:

> smuggling? alternate urban trees with drought,
> uploaded from templates. science fictionelle?
> tomorrow's psychedelic literature will scheme,
> will be in cahoots with its readership,

will select the most special page from a beloved book,
easily mailed to all those countries with their "elections"
and "coalitions." if it were possible to read I would be enchanted.
but so expensive, must we print more money? more books?

climbing their leaves and branches until
they are foreclosed upon to be made new.
thank you for this, but are we ready? it feels not
uncommon to getting a new suitcase.

to premier musicians playing for free outside
subway stations, and no one with the time
to stop and listen. not enough time

not enough djs.
not enough bodyguards.
not world enough. no time.

me laugh me processed food
me potato jackets with "bacon" bits
me mozzarella stix for days

to stay undone. braced from
the ultra one-dimensional to enter
the New Reality. caught hold through the door
up in my face.

next time send someone more
st. tropez than outer borough.
never go into the city, nevermore.
it's not what it once was.

I lied all along.
I'm in bed with revolution
the only system for everyone: mass action
is beautiful process, believes in us

despite media blackout. ecstasy meme
grabs officers' unknown essential selves for
the richest man on this earth. discovers addiction
unrelated to production or consumption:

a failed attempt to shift. to smash apart
perception itself, set and setting ever more.
there is no I in fuck you.
beyond essentially awake to ignorance, bliss.

a story about space-time and collective global
redemption: a miracle. an intimation of understanding—
the doorway is the gate welcoming home severed
connections to the numinous construction of reality.

impartial

1. a real rain

had us.
   some dream.
   just disgraced contents,
unknown foil, filled one city
     field once foliage.
leaky expectation
      bounds rough space.

a limited amount
     of know now protection.
    always think sparingly—
  do still.
   life renews necessary
decay falls,
  become a real harvest.

2. an unexpected market

check conditional, circumstantial limits to power,
action environment at capacity. essentials

extenuate only remembrance: forgotten through
insulation, current opposition. flow forward.

compelling nature by making fit force of attraction:
were you intentional? cloaking radiance. sink heat.

bound by potent spells, enchantments, causal shifts?
there, there, still   distant may actually happen.

3. I'm your biggest fan

clocks tick too slowly.
unreliability lights hurt her world eyes—

atmospheric irritant. literalized.
hasty investigation of a very bad dream.

here, try one of these—
believe what I see: integrated shock—

doorways forced—
one with its defects.

your face rings a bell

liquid means falling
from heights
of witherdom.
peace, he said,
is the gentle dove
re-introduced to the colony.

having picked up a native
language from other birds,
pronunciation deteriorates
over time to survive
new habitats.
even in this rain.

survive and flourish.
fluctuate—
three times in a day
to be received.
three times
under arched hallways.

weigh so light
from flee through the transom
through the yellow light
to superstars.
and superstar debris
to crash. to land.

any moment woke
wonder to riot, breath
brawl: *ha ha ha ha ha*
to slow down.
if that doesn't slow you down,
the river certainly will.

electrified bog,
kiss boulevard.
kiss pavement,
lamp post.
hand to door.
name with face.

space encapsulated
contained consciousness
and ayahuasca-aided visuals:

                                           that.

                                           bucket.

                                           there.

                                           these.

                                           walls.

they

want.

to

be.

with

me.

my visits to the other side
are well documented.
mine *and* yours.
both of ours,
entwined among our
grape-leaved loggia,
ancient marble bench
upon which we now rest.

as real as it seems,
this revolution.
how to rise up
every day?
slip this slipping
movement. form

a proper shut to
oppression in the form
of stress fractures,
exacerbated.
this blind
I mean mute

every day.
this tired slipping
from glass heights.
wired for repo
belief
repossessed belief

my life

we.

most my land.

tear song
wiped dripping
from lips

with the full chieftain,
the slice of life-giving
flavor. dosed that
fucking hole in the wall
protecting a hole in the wall?
what was going to happen?

them bee to honey.
flavorized. faster
than the speed
of light. most of it
would burn up
on re-entry or land

safely in the ocean
and the odds,
the staggering odds
against it,
it will never happen.
nothing's going to change.

how

could

it?

and

why?

. . . .

all is not yet lost

. . . .

to protect us

take us down together
joined form torn letters
armed around the absolute.
admit it. note the theoretical
damp: village equilibrium.
language we just made up

not a pidgin anymore—
together parts confusion waves
our built-in thanks to sway
to enter cosmic crash
ashore from watered chance
side to side a bird like grand,

fingered. glove lost, running free
to gloat to under likened
chop and protect us how magic turns
our heads sharply into animal
knives. lost skin takes eyes.
my will become rock.

indigenous silence

hunted glorification
will haunt the tale as
group of tongue and space
backs wandering stars' vernacular.

that quickening is complicit.
science separate from story
disappoints, addicts to difficulty
positioned cloud up

holds the weather to understand—
I used to could,
from first light.
a new zodiac introduce

my devised constellations
from device. stars where
bodies distrust discretion,
magnetic as true.

indigenous science,
our struggle are evermore
lost are struggle fundamental
of related stories, kin.

impossible lies

wild control be our control
to desire up
presumptuous songs
of impossible lies ahead

what can I tomb from rising
and transform all.
is there any feeling?
can there be

below the way
harmony kept time
with keeping endeavor
I will guide the stars

got protected
and so beloved
and myself
of cares taken,

I now self her.
of care taken can
a grown-assed woman
survive longing?

danger? sacrifice
wonder to be sense.
let us return to the feast.
the fire woods.

laughter led to find
"Spontaneous" "Adventure"
and "Excitement."
make we feel positive danger.

feel them up by the river
(or what passes for rivers
in these parts) victory.
triumph. bait. lure.

makes years so many
for real. true deceptions
feel nothing of shallow.
of disappointment, so absurd.

downed attention
where hosts of admirers
need an audience. soul delicate.
believed to begin so very badly.

decolonized

corrected course embodied
decoded place: our social
forms as elaborate stitches:

them partially funded
them happy valley
into fragments dispensed

with myopic clouds and trees
both memorying embroiderment,
navigating necessary

alleviation of alleviation.
endangered stewardship
taken in hand. device

information bloated device
relevant to impertinent
cooperation left space,

such arrogance, such rudeness
on the world inflicted
infinite yoga studios and

bells, wind chimes, bell neem
everywhere, filling cracks in
indian lilac hopes of restoring intimacy.

I am the man

the god of fuck matures good fortune's river
run through a machine house of bone structure.
wind foundation, a playful, cheerful fear
inside waters' sunken ship formula for success itself
the self of the sparrow wing the golden dove's bowl
and plastic spoon felt pleased attached the man's
undercurrent of disbelief as an engine's roar in a paved lot
glittering anger and the shattered glass of disappointment.

exile soaked

glorified wild and free but fenced
off body shade field challenge
a healing leaved body prolonging
attachment's shallow, dismal
and staggering present. injured, ill,
preoccupied with your arms,
with so forth and ceasing.
particularities bond river influence
to snow fronds, vast and opposing
staying—the sea polarized
denial of limitations
soaked with sense of exile.

theory notes

sum of us
buried debts

of ritualized
connection

coming certain
heart from being

undone with me.
the foundry

where being
done of certain

loves getting
stone heavy

of massive.
body stone

and wig stone;
mesmerism

in the head
and the incessant

pounding.
they don't warn you

of how loud,
how lucky

when the job is done,
turning us divisive—

all desire,
all design.

solved equation

measurements note an increased
production of possibility—
detect acceleration. excitement
at this is wrong thinking.

standards that underlie ignorance
cannot embarrass—
light becomes everything
heavy. everything thought.

continuum loosened thinking to
consequent measurement, wondrous
truth. the weakness of will
and live equations—

form following concentrated
energy to solution. to amazement.
turned out regional accents
through warped dramatics—

spread the very universe.
space be not the same as space-time.
stuck in geometries, we can
never interact. always true.

our viewpoint is
the dimensional light
outside the floating world,
stuck appearance.

to get around neighbor complaints

neighborhood space debris: asteroids, satellites,
dead transmitters offer no complaints, are the fire
of heaven become self-aware around trees
disguised as transmission towers, downed.
that scent interpretation to cover the earth,
the ionosphere. bouncing off sky waves—
across the purest glass. a lightning strike
of suspicion connects inner shield with passing bodies,
a vampire tap. signals, echoing the old days—
problems, noise. our work others each.
immediately recognized in the visible light.
we go, tremendously high. to turn terrain toward the sun.

machines at work

despised metal makes light the only remaining routine

peopled walks are a swallowed sky, bordered, stolen.

torn, wrenching rejoices at difficulty.

blank walls communicate silenced fire

to celebrate the despondent, dispassionate,

freestanding mettle. still living, synthetic:

an unmarked hillside or populated city equally

the underbelly of a forgotten fertile plain.

logics night repentant.

a slowed crawl, fuels forgetting.

landscaped

moving oppressive
fantasies at play
driven by scratched
win, caress rock.
stab, hammer.
small motors control
my mechanism: spoon,
shoe, suitcase.
mercury, cold
the handicraft world
miles its age as
a vertebrate's poise
before collapse, a
shimmering wake
boundaries the plastic mind,
fetters open thinking—
marks bed sheets with
cello stains here upended.
floating ponds the wall.
variable dimensions
achieve results.

wow, loot!
(w00t!)

concrete smoothed water
calls liquid at night
about her voice
to lull into forgetting
and confusion from
the drawn swords
of absolute clarity.
wing crushed hands

entirely justified victory
of poisoned hearts hatched
great shadows—boom field the bois.
long time robot camouflaged
rage as pre-formatted entertainment
from each big box store long
way from the portable
ballast called home.

as above

the frightened pull trip
tops taught silence. taught technique
embodied sugar stops. not yet.
burnished through a series of searings,
muscle spasms. series of rubber bands
and there—metal wires. tightened ropes.
or sometimes, when lenient, cardboard
backing. whalebone inserts. to bend into
shape, to pull back. withhold. straighten
the curved. tuck in the overflowing. tighten,
tauten what is loose, unstructured.

must border control and barrier this with
all scientific know now. am too large feet
and too loose of belly. full flatten and fold.

will out

customary. with rivers,
cleaning success is everything
run from claiming triumph's
flung stone: truth always be out—
drunk on the very mechanics—

of procedures' quiet throne.
unfair to selective, brute
force systems solvent to shore.
they end. united font strength

evasion started to be
my light, my source of english
turned back at the junction
to eat promise—
a huge relief despite

still some hero thing:
dark loam converted to silt
to question. to start to expect
video of scent trail. exhaust
triumphant trumps disaster.

luck in a hurry

our square of orange change
moved to encircle: I am right

and you are ultra-right.
drawn from bare bark.

think stick thin branch
unbroken through winter—

the cold budded. bring bloom
from sun gray sky blew

here to protect the people
and song for the come together.

we car wrathful.
in our very own bodies

this is the most potentially
everyone. against all odds.

we are not easy
to find and wonderful.

increasingly great, this
is my favorite. dinner.

and dancing. we love.
to dancing. to music.

we are bringing everything
to cultivate qualities, we do.

stormed capital

total alimentation
articulates our
single history-decisive our
material arrival at
a fruitful marketplace
passionate newspaper
affairs work my
optimism, preoccupy
daily hopes for a government
of the heart. more fitted
responsibilities exactly
three blocks from necessary.
the family, town life
important conditions
adapted to trial
levels, staged questions
protected parts of a
fierce wind, a driving
rain. just become just.
true danger could be life
ordered to follow
staid, safe.
steeped in plenty
with water and food,
shelter considered
for ease of evacuation.

(see flooding)
we will bank.

overflow nothing.
isolated, political
become stormed, capital

not an error of the oracle

well water joined freezing to rise up
as island. forbid pleasure-indulged
pain: thorned, barbed—blurred, lost.
ignited to receive and inflict. eating
through constellations reignites the brilliantly
vicious. torment bound tomorrow
morning's slippery infiltration: multiverse
expands. if a bond of live exists,
no distance keeps. captivated
by a flat land incapable of more.

don't miss your water

crisis connects.
got served
unknowable variables
false collapse
of personal
history—victim
indicates refusal.
disavowal.
pride in tolerance
for poison
capacity incites
white riot,
an unwelcome companion—
destabilization's alchemical
necessity: the arousing.
consider the well
bone dry.

non-hostile takeover

appreciate the wall
conspiring to arid
asphalt, metal.

glass and steel nothing.
wary surface world
still capable—in need.

a vast well within
the inner courtyard
at the speed of handwriting.

if a bond of love exists—
free engagement
with the miraculous present.

intrinsic underestimation engine:
tonight's the night!
let's change the sheets.

obtain the love of the people,
in a hard-won settlement: capacity
for the depressingly ordinary.

Betsy Fagin is the author of *Names Disguised* (Make Now Press, 2014), *Poverty Rush* (Three Sad Tigers, 2011), *the science seemed so solid* (dusie kollektiv, 2011), *Belief Opportunity* (Big Game Books Tinyside, 2008), *Rosemary Stretch* (dusie e/chap, 2006) and *For every solution there is a problem* (Open 24 Hours, 2003).

She received degrees in literature and creative writing from Vassar College and Brooklyn College and completed her MLS degree in Information Studies at the University of Maryland where she was an American Library Association Spectrum Scholar. In 2011, Betsy served as Librarian for the People's Library of Occupy Wall Street through the consensus of the New York City General Assembly. She was a writer-in-residence at the Lower Manhattan Cultural Council during 2012-13.

Deepest thanks to all the friends, lovers, family members, allies, enemies, perfect strangers and unseen forces who conspired with me in the creation of these poems. I'm forever grateful. Go, team!

Thank you to the editors and publishers of the following journals in which some of these poems first appeared:

About Place (decolonized, exile soaked, *from* Narcissus and
    Echo, it's going to be all right, never not broken)
Alice Blue Review (glass heart)
Big Bell (all I wanna do, no, this will never really work but
    here's why)
Brooklyn Rail (don't miss your water, graceful degradation,
    impartial)
Critical Quarterly (stormed capital)
Little Red Leaves (landscaped)
Open Letters Monthly (new old forest: infrastructure)
The Recluse (luck in a hurry, non-hostile takeover, theory
    notes, to get around neighbor complaints, to protect us)
Spiral Orb (machines at work)
Spooky Boyfriend (I am the man)
Upstairs at Duroc (fail-safe, resolved)
Vlak (solved equation)

decolonized was published as a broadside from Belladonna in 2014.

solved equation was published as a broadside from the Center for the Book Arts, NYC in 2013.

green press INITIATIVE

Belladonna Books is committed to preserving ancient forests and natural resources. We elected to print this title on 30% postconsumer recycled paper, processed chlorine-free. As a result, we have saved:

0 Trees (40' tall and 6-8" diameter)
1 Million BTUs of Total Energy
64 Pounds of Greenhouse Gases
348 Gallons of Wastewater
23 Pounds of Solid Waste

Belladonna Books made this paper choice because our printer, Thomson-Shore, Inc., is a member of Green Press Initiative, a nonprofit program dedicated to supporting authors, publishers, and suppliers in their efforts to reduce their use of fiber obtained from endangered forests.

For more information, visit www.greenpressinitiative.org

Environmental impact estimates were made using the Environmental Defense Paper Calculator. For more information visit: www.edf.org/papercalculator